Suzuki®

VIOLA SCHOOL

Volume 3
Viola Part
Revised Edition

© 2009, 1999, 1983 Dr. Shinichi Suzuki
Sole publisher for the entire world except Japan:
Summy-Birchard, Inc.
Exclusive print rights administered by Alfred Publishing Co., Inc.
All rights reserved.   Printed in USA.

ISBN 0-7579-2475-1
ISBN-13: 978-0-7579-2475-0

The Suzuki name, logo and wheel device
are trademarks of Dr. Shinichi Suzuki
used under exclusive license by Summy-Bichard, Inc.

INTRODUCTION

This transposition of the SUZUKI VIOLIN SCHOOL makes available to the viola student the carefully structured repertoire of The Suzuki Method™ — a method that teaches basic playing skills and develops listening and memorizing ability through the playing of beautiful music.

Regardless of the age of the student, it is hoped that Dr. Suzuki's principles of learning by listening, training the memory, and concentrating on producing a beautiful tone will be observed. Remember that ability develops after a composition has been learned — in the mastering process. The practice suggestions emphasize the need to isolate technical and musical problems, and encourage the teacher to use all the opportunities inherent in the repertoire for orderly growth toward mastery of the instrument.

Doris Preucil

STUDY POINTS FOR VOLUME 3

1. Have the children listen daily to the recordings of the music they are currently studying. This listening helps them make rapid progress.

2. Tonalization should always be included at each lesson and should be a part of the daily practice at home.

3. Constant attention should be given to accurate intonation.

4. In Volume 3, particular emphasis should be placed on the study of phrasing. Children should learn to end each phrase pianissimo.

SUGGESTIONS FOR TONE PRODUCTION

It is best to hold the bow with the right corner of the thumb tip placed opposite the middle and ring fingers. The power of the thumb pressing at this location is an important factor in tone production.

The student should always play with the bow held firmly so that the tip of the bow remains steady. A superior tone depends on this bow hold.

CONTENTS

Transcribed for Viola and Piano by Doris Preucil

Tonalization

Each lesson should begin with tonalization. Tonalization should be
stressed constantly in order to improve and refine the tone.

At the lesson use both bowing alternatives ⊓ and ∨ for
beginning each exercise.

S. C. Foster

Exercises for Changing Strings

These exercises should be taught at each lesson, and practiced very
slowly at first. Increase the speed as the child's ability develops.
As the speed increases, the bow strokes should become shorter.

1
Gavotte

P. Martini

*See practice suggestions on page 22.

2 Minuet

Minuet I

J. S. Bach

Allegretto

mf con grazia

3
Gavotte in G Minor

J. S. Bach

*See practice suggestions on page 23.

Observe the crescendos and diminuendos by controlling the varying bow
speeds (slower bow stroke at the indication p, and faster stroke at f).
Practice finishing each phrase beautifully, pianissimo, using a short and soft stroke.

Tonalization
G minor (melodic) scale

Try to make all the tones have the resonance of the open strings.

Note that the 6th and 7th tones are each raised one half-step in the
ascending scale, but appear as in the key signature in the descending scale.

4
Humoresque

A. Dvořák

✗ Preliminary Practice

Set bow at middle. Use a very short bow stroke.
Keep the bow on the string during the rest.

5
Gavotte

Jean Becker

poco rit.

C Major Scale in Thirds

C Major Triad Exercise

In every bar except bar 7, the first and third notes are a *perfect fifth* apart, and can be fingered directly across from the other. In bar 7, they create a *diminished fifth*, with the second finger one-half step lower on the higher string. The diminished fifth occurs in every key between the 7th and 4th tones of the scale.

Chromatic Scales

Slide the finger without moving the hand.

6
Minuet in D

W. A. Mozart, K. 439 B
D. Preucil

*See practice suggestions on page 24.

0243S

7
Gavotte
(from Orchestral Suite No. 3)

J. S. Bach

Gavotte I

Gavotte II

8

Bourrée

J. S. Bach

EV scale

Bourrée II

Trill Exercise: Play with a strong tone. Use a short bow stroke.

Chord Exercises: Play with the same resonant sound as that produced when tuning.
In practicing chords, the forefinger should be lifted off the bow. The bow should be
held and controlled principally by the 3rd and 4th fingers.

Practice Suggestions

(Gavotte by Martini)

1. Bowing: Place bow slightly above middle and use entire arm for the repeated up-bows. Remember to use good bow distribution. Quick long bows can be used in loud passages. Use slower and lighter strokes for phrase endings.

2. Fingering: Review the C minor tonalization and the three finger patterns below.

Practice pulling 1st finger back without the hand in this exercise which prepares measure 28. Try it two ways: both holding and picking up the 2nd finger.

3. Memory: The sections of Gavotte have been designated in the music by the use of letters. Note that a varying section always alternates with the A section. Compare B with D, and C with E, to see how they differ. Practice each section separately until independently secure.

(Minuet)

1. Please refer to practice suggestions in Suzuki Viola Volume 1, Minuet No. 3, for the C major portion.

2. At measure 50, note change of key to C minor. Review this finger pattern, keeping 1st and 2nd fingers spread when using 3rd and 4th fingers. Try to keep space open all the way to the base of the fingers.

3. C melodic minor scale: Note that the 6th and 7th tones are each raised in the ascending scale, but appear as in the key signature in the descending scale.

(Gavotte in G minor)

1. Section B is fingered in second position. Shifting exercises are found in Suzuki Viola Volume 2. Try this game: drop arm during rests, and replace finger precisely in tune. See example below

2. The alternate fingering in 3rd position is advised in section C. In measures 36 and 38, shift up to 3rd position on 1st finger. Always shift on finger last used.

(Minuet in D)

Match the pitches carefully.

Avoid curling 4th finger.

(Gavotte from Orchestral Suite No. 3)

1) Practice holding fingers down as indicated by connecting lines.

2) Use alternating bowings.

Exercises are for practice in both holding and lifting fingers. Try to avoid curling 4th finger when placing 3rd finger. Repeat each measure several times.

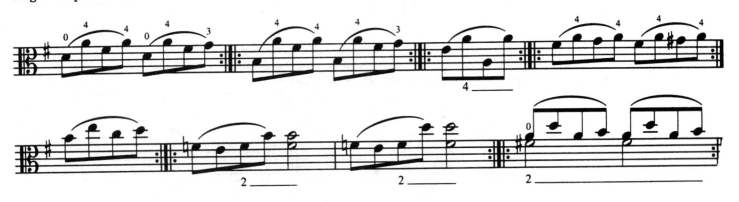

(Bourrée)

1st pos.   2nd pos.   1st pos.

When shifting from an open string feel the distance of the shift in the hand (between thumb and first finger).

1st   2nd   1st   2nd